DREAM BUILD SUCCESS

PLAN, PRODUCE, AND PROFIT TO SIX FIGURES

LASHANDA D. GARY

Copyright © 2017 LaShanda Gary

All rights reserved.

Dream Build Success © 2016 LaShanda Gary. All Rights Reserved.
No part of this publication may be reproduced, stored in a retrieval system, or
transmitted, in any form or in any means – by electronic, mechanical,
photocopying, recording or other- wise – without prior written permission.

Graphics and Media Copyright © 2016 by LaShanda Gary All rights reserved.
This book or any portion thereof may not be reproduced or used in any manner whatsoever without the express written permission of the publisher except for the use of brief quotations in a book review.

Printed in the United States of America First Printing, 2016

G.L.A. Executive Services, LLC P.O. Box 764
Rosenberg, Texas 77471

www.DreamBuildSuccess.com

ISBN-13:978-1519740298

ISBN-10:1519740298

CONTENTS

	Acknowledgments	Pg. 5
	Introduction	Pg. 7
1	Questions	Pg. 9
2	Real Business	Pg. 15
3	Risk	Pg. 25
4	Start Now	Pg. 31
5	Plan	Pg. 41
6	Get Paid	Pg. 61
7	Productivity Planner	Pg. 171
8	Reference:	Pg. 185
	About the Author	Pg. 187

ACKNOWLEDGMENTS

I am blessed to be surrounded by amazing people who support and believe in me each day.

I dedicate this book to the goal getter, passion pursuing, and purpose driven women around the world. It is time to finally get your life and success together. You have taken the first step of activating your next dimension of success by simply picking this book up. The modern-day woman who is dedicated to learning, growing, and expanding beyond what she can see. She is a brilliant thinker, savvy business woman, with ginormous faith. To the teenager who is a hidden treasure.

To the special people in my life that have prayed me through during this journey, encouraged me at my lowest points. And encouraged me to stand on faith. Thank You! To my family, friends, parents, and Dream Team. God, Bless you!

My husband, Abret, who inspires me each day to do the impossible. Your love and encouragement are priceless. Thank you for making my life more inspiring than I ever imagined. I love you! Luke 1:37, with God nothing shall be impossible.

LaShanda Gary

INTRODUCTION

At some point, the fun definitely left my life and now I'm committed to giving you the truth as I know it and as I learned myself on this entrepreneurial journey. Biggest lesson CEOs- Nothing is going to move until you do.

It is so easy to find reasons for our reasons on why we can't do things. Money is usually the biggest villain. But, if you really think about it, in private, when it really comes down to it, is money the real problem? Have you specified what you need money for exactly? When I ask Dream Build Success members or clients this question, it is AMAZING that about ninety-eight percent of them have no idea what they actually need the money for. They just knew that they couldn't move forward because of the lack of funds. Is that you too? Don't be ashamed. Many of us get so comfortable with our excuses, they become our friends. When someone offers us a way to remove them, we feel lonely, unsure, and get scared of open space opportunity.

Technology has given us an edge. The small businesses, the new entrepreneur, the scrappy start-up we all have an edge. We can build some amazing things that take no money, but plenty of hustle, wittiness, and risk taking. Basically, us getting off our bottoms and using all our tools and taking advantage of the opportunities available to us.

I spent six months of study just to see if there was information easily found to start and build a business, and I did find it. No, it wasn't quick. Yes, it took several hours of reading and some hours writing it. Not only did I find information, I compiled it in a nice and neat package for you in this book.

So, I admonish you to build your dream life, a big bank account and teach others once you understand and maximize your profitability.

GO BIG OR GO HOME.

CHAPTER 1

ASK QUESTIONS

"Every level of creativity starts with a question."

- LaShanda D. Gary

When we think of the world's greatest innovators, voices, or collaborators, we tend to remember a select few whose innovations and speeches quite literally changed the world. We often think of the greats, Oprah Winfrey, Steve Jobs, or Martin Luther King, Jr. And yet, every day we take advantage of the words and devices created by millions of investors who are not and may never be a household name, but truly make the world a better place. They are young, they are moms, dads, sisters, brothers, and labor-saving ideas that literally give us the quality of life.

This is the start of your think tank moment. You definitely want to grab a pen and a cup of tea, so you can prepare yourself to answer the hard questions. We have to start with the questions that you definitely need to ask yourself.

1. How committed am I?

This one trumps all the rest, and getting to a meaningful answer involves some serious self-honesty. Commitment comes from motivation---the fuel you need to get really good at something.

Now take a few minutes to ask yourself the following questions and prepare to write what you learn or hear.

2. What motivates you?

Leaving a legacy? Funding your kids' education? The

second home near salt water? The need to make a difference? Sheer pride? There are no feel-good answers, only authentic ones.

3. What's my value proposition?

Every company, project, and employee should have a value prop---preferably a clear and measurable one---though plenty is wanting. Chew on yours a bit. In a question, later in the book, I'll show you why the answer may not be what you think it is.

4. Am I clearly communicating my value proposition?

You should be able to explain---in three sentences describe your value proposition and why customers need what you're selling. If you can't, you're in big trouble: The reality is (and don't take it personally) no one really cares about what you do. You have to make them care. This is as important as offering something worth caring about, which is why it's not folded into the previous question.

PowerPoint presentations are nice (actually, most aren't), but you should know your value prop so cold and be able to deliver it so compellingly, that you can grab someone's attention in the amount of time it takes to ride an elevator with them. Whatever you do, don't freight your elevator pitch with meaningless jargon like "robust solution," "leveraging best practices."

Matt Hunckler knows the power of a good, quick pitch. A few years ago, he founded Verge to connect tech startups in Indianapolis with software developers and investors. Every month Hunckler organizes a 200-person gathering, sponsored by tech companies and venture capital firms, where entrepreneurs make their case. (Attendance fee: $10).

Presenters get all of five minutes to cover their value prop, the size of their potential market, any unique technology they've developed, and the quality of their management team. Says Huckler: "If the presenter is still talking at the 5-minute mark, all 200 people start a slow clap" to move them off the stage.

5. Clarity is essential

Clarity is the ultimate command, and if you want results you've never had you need to get 100 percent clear on what you want. Only when you take full responsibility for your current reality can you change it. Minimalism is a great way to run your business, and a great way to run your life. Get rid of the messes and noise in your head and figure out who you are, what you want and what you must give up to get there.

CHAPTER 2

TALK ABOUT BUSINESS

In this chapter, you will learn the next step to building your six-figure income. You have to ask yourself if you're working on an expensive hobby or a real business.

Is my product/service a real business?

This is a bombshell question. Many people have expensive hobbies they like to call businesses. What's better: one hundredth of 1% of a $100 billion market, or 25% of a $40 million market? Of course, they're the same in dollar terms, but for whatever reasons capturing that thin slice of a massive pie might be much harder and less profitable than owning a fatter slice of a small one. As John De Puy, CEO of Oaktree Ventures, a San Diego-based venture capital firm, put it: "Define and dominate---that's the secret sauce."

The not-so-secret sauce is "scale." Scalable businesses produce the next widget at minimal additional expense. Think software: Once Microsoft developed the code for its Windows operating system, the incremental cost of distributing each additional copy was minuscule. Service businesses, on the other hand, aren't as scalable because the need for people generally increases with each additional client.

The lust for scale led to the tech wreck of 2000, but hope and hype are alive and kicking. The latest headline stealer: Pinterest, a social media site that lets visitors collect and share images on virtual pin boards. In nine months, the site attracted 18 million unique visitors per month; such scale is truly remarkable considering that new users have to bother requesting an invite to start pinning. While Pinterest has yet to demonstrate a viable business model (the site is free), that didn't stop it from luring $27 million in venture capital.

What differentiates my product from the competition?

This one and the three that follow---all having to do with understanding and maintaining competitive advantage---come from the playbook of Michael Porter, a professor at Harvard Business School and famed corporate strategist.

Having an advantage means delivering more value than your competitors do, in the form of lower prices (Wal-Mart), better design (Apple), instant gratification (Google), or some other tangible benefit. If someone tells you his or her company has no competition, that person is 1) naïve, 2) silly, or 3) insane. (That's why, as part of last year's search for "America's Most Promising Companies," Forbes asked contenders to provide descriptions of up to three majors competitors; companies that didn't answer were discounted or discarded.

Back to the warning in question number two: While your product may sell, what you think makes it special may have little to do with what customers actually crave. Misdiagnosing that mismatch can lead to all sorts of bad strategic decisions. A fast-food chain can sell more milkshakes by figuring out why people were buying them in the first place. It turned out that the answer had nothing to do with how thick and delicious the shakes were; it had to do with the "job" the shakes were being "hired" for.

You should take a few minutes to write down a strategy to create a product or service that will help add an additional thousand dollars to your income on a daily, weekly, and monthly. Let's do the math, you have to at least bring home $1,923.07 every week to hit your $100,000⁺ goal. Or, you can break it down to $8,333.33 every month to break even at $100,000. So, if you want to shatter the glass ceiling of the six-figure mark you probably should aim for at minimum, $140,000 in gross profits.

I can already hear you saying, this lady is nuts. How am I going to make that much income without a plan, products, or a process in place to implement this, "MEGA PLAN!"

Well, I'm overjoyed that you have your thinking cap on. In the next section of the book, you will learn some key ingredients to your success.

How much power do my customers have?

Customers are good; crutches are not. Delphi Automotive, the giant auto parts supplier, went bankrupt in 2005 despite generating $26 billion in annual revenue. A big reason: It served a few large customers who held so much sway that they could demand price cuts each passing year. (Delphi has since reorganized and went public.)

Understanding your customers is critical when it comes to buying power. This is something I learned very well while managing my thirteen million dollar departments in the retail industry. It was simple, if I didn't understand what the buyer wanted, we did not profit.

How much power do my suppliers have?

As with buyers, the more you rely on any one vendor, the tougher the terms he'll eventually extract. That's why America's widening trade deficit with China is a big concern. China "supplies" the U.S. with capital so that Americans can keep buying its exports. If that trade gap grows large enough, the cost of renting that capital will spike, crimping America's ability to pay for other stuff like education, infrastructure, and scientific research.

Does my business have a trench around it?

If you're smart enough to spy a profitable business opportunity, rest assured competition isn't far behind.

Or, instead of a direct competitor, maybe a substitute technology will come along (think what digital film did to Kodak). Some moats---patented technology, a storied brand---are more difficult to cross than others, but someone will always find a way to do the job faster, cheaper and better.

Are you confident?

Insecurities will destroy you, while real confidence will take you to a level very few attain. An interesting thing happens when you start to gain clarity. Your confidence follows. If you don't have confidence, you will always find a way to lose. Everything you accomplish is based on the confidence you have in yourself and your ability to "make it happen." The bigger the goals, the bigger the challenges.

You must realize the moment you go after your biggest goals, obstacles will show up. They are there to test your character and faith, and to see if you are serious about your goals. The person with the most confidence always wins. When I got clear on the actions needed to start thriving, I felt my motivation and energy elevate. These days, the only security you have is the confidence in yourself and your ability to make things happen.

Shifting your circle of influence.

There comes a point in your life when you realize who really matters, who never did and who always will. Once really matters, who never did and who always will. Once you get clear on who you are and what you want, you must re-evaluate your *Circle of Influence*.

Who you associate with is who you become. The term "role model" is not used enough in our society. It's extremely important to have role models. A role model will raise your standards. A role model will not let you get complacent. Finding a role model or mentor will spark your mind because they are playing the game at a higher level than you are.

If you hang around five confident people, you will be the sixth.

If you hang around five intelligent people, you will be the sixth.

If you hang around five millionaires, you will be the sixth.

If you hang around five idiots, you will be the sixth.

If you hang around five broke people, you will be the sixth.

It's inevitable.

Such a simple concept, but what a difference it can make on your performance and business. There's no faster way to advance into the top 5 percent of your industry than this. Yet, most people don't do it. I challenge you to find those people because you'll become a lot like the people you spend the most time with. Their belief systems, their ways of being and their attitudes are contagious. Once you elevate your peer group, your standards will follow.

CHAPTER 3

WHY RISK IT

There are all kinds of initiatives, from modest lifestyle businesses to publicly traded behemoths. The larger they are, the greater the risk---in dollars, time, reputation and ego. Be honest about how much you think you can stomach without making emotionally charged decisions or developing a headache.

Not an adventurer? That doesn't mean you can't build a sizable business. Just ask Maryjo Cohen, chief executive of National Presto Industries, an eclectic manufacture of kitchen appliances, bullets, and diapers. For years Cohen stored cash and government bonds---in 1999, as oceans of cheap money sloshing about, National Presto's cash and securities accounted for 80% of its assets. When stock analysts pressured Cohen to hit quarterly earnings targets, she told them to get lost. "For all her wealth, Cohen lives with her mom in the three-bedroom, poured-concrete house in Eau Clair, Wisconsin where she grew up," reported *Forbes* in October 2009. "She flies coach, stays at Holiday Inns...and has yet to upgrade from dial-up service for her home computer." Cohen got the last laugh: When the market turned, National Presto's pristine balance sheet allowed it to make timely acquisitions and add equipment.

In the years past, the company has netted $48 million on $431 million in sales; since 1999 its stock price has doubled, to $72 a share, while the S&P 500 advanced just 4%.

Whatever your appetite for risk, there will be setbacks. Expect them, adjust and move on. As the saying goes: "If your uniform isn't dirty, you didn't play."

What's the *smartest* way to fund my goal?

Not all investment capital is created equal. Generally, using your own is expensive but clean; using someone else's is cheaper but messier. Getting the most out of limited capital takes brains, imagination and boldness. Brad Harlow, chief executive of Physio Sonics, maker of blood-flow monitors in Bellevue, WA., nearly folded up shop twice a few years ago. To keep his startup afloat, Harlow pitted his investors---including two giant medical-device rivals, Johnson & Johnson and Medtronic---against each other in the capital pecking order and gave neither first rights to buy him out. Now that's brash.

Then there's Alan Martin, fresh-faced founder of Campus Books Rentals (CampusBookRentals.com (a member of Forbes' America's Most Promising Companies list). In the teeth of the 2008 financial crisis, Martin quit his job and loaded up six credit cards---simultaneously, so the card companies wouldn't balk---to raise $250,000 to launch an online textbook-rental company. Oh, and his wife was 4-months pregnant at the time. NO EXCUSES!

There are textbooks galore on the merits of debt, equity and everything in between. The point of these examples and countless others: **Where there's a will, there's a financial way.**

Am I outsourcing the right tasks?

This is a precarious question you should definitely be asking yourself. Being bogged down by unnecessary task, obligations, and meaningless projects will make you miss opportunities that only happen by showing up.

For an example, if you own a shirt or an apparel line. Why would we buy imported shirts and shoes made by poorly educated workers in Bangladesh? Because our local fashion school, with savvy interns, could work for minimal or even free and also know how to design and manufacture apparel.

But sometimes "what you do best" isn't the only criteria for choosing which tasks to keep in-house. On the flip side, you might think peddling new merchandise or products requires a gifted in-house sales staff. Outsource the sales function. Listen, star salespeople have their own interests at heart, not their employer's." I once read that quote, in Forbes many years ago.

I totally believe that's right: many companies carry no direct sales force *and* he operates globally." Sometimes the price may be will double once it's ready to distribute, but it is definitely worth the try.

Who is my role model?
Somewhere, someone is "doing it right" in your industry. Investors (and employers) want to know you've thought hard about who those companies are and why specifically they are setting the standard you aim to beat. You have to find a role model, in human form. Many times, we look at syndicated television and try to identify with characters on the latest reality show. This will not work, you have to find

a role model quickly. As a Christian woman, I always seek God for wisdom while looking for a role model.

You have to build your foundational core to connect with like-minded people or hire someone to teach you the skills that are needed to implement your goals. Try focusing on meeting new people, visit new places, and actively participate in your six-figure plan.

CHAPTER 4

START NOW

While earning six figures doesn't mean what it used to, it is still a very admirable (and achievable) goal. So how do you go about reaching this significant salary milestone? Let's discuss.

1. Start now

If you are just beginning your career it is unlikely you will be able to earn $100,000+ per year today. However, now is the time to focus on developing the points below. By the time, you are twenty years into your career and earning half of what you should be it is often too late to make up the difference.

Any profession is a relatively slow accumulation of experience and qualifications The sooner you can master the following points the better positioned you will be in the [near] future to command a higher salary than your less capable peers.

2. Develop your skills

The definition of insanity is doing the same thing over and over again and expecting a different result. The same is true for your career. If you are doing the same thing every day and expecting a higher salary it is unlikely to happen.

What can you do today that will make you more valuable tomorrow? Increasing your "hard skills" is a relatively easy first step to implement.

Hard skills examples:
- Design skill
- Tech knowledge
- Industry awareness
- Data analysis
- Qualifications
- Degrees
- Purpose
- Verbal Skillset
- Project Management

However, it is just as important to develop your "soft skills".

Soft skills examples
- Communication skills
- Leadership skills
- Adaptability and flexibility
- Problem-solving
- Decision-making
- Creativity
- Team-working
- Time management skills

- Willingness to learn

These typically take longer to perfect so you need to start now. Focus on one topic per day and try to tweak one aspect of your work day or routine to improve one of these skills.

3. Reduce the stress of others

In a recent interview with Mark Cuban, he stated one of the keys to success is to *"reduce the stress of your co-workers"*. When you are at work, reduce the stress of your colleges and supervisors. If you can reduce other people's stress, those people will gravitate towards you. You will be seen as the leader and your colleagues will eventually want to work for you.

4. Be the best

Without a doubt, specialization is key to a high salary. In other words, "what do you do better than anyone else?" This can be as broad as expertise in a certain building typology or as specific as airport BIM Management (who, by the way, can make substantial incomes).

5. Take responsibility

As the saying goes, "don't ask permission just ask for forgiveness". Responsibility is not something that is just handed out, you need to take the initiative and go above and beyond what is expected.

You can't be at the bottom of the pyramid and expect to be well compensated. If you want to climb the pay scale you must challenge yourself by taking on more responsibility, which will ultimately translate into more income. This doesn't necessarily mean working long hours but you need to be as efficient and productive as possible.

If you are just beginning your career, start small. Take on the task of leading a small portion of a project. By proving to others that you are reliable and dependable you will be rewarded over time.

7. Have regular performance reviews

This is an opportunity for you to discuss with your partner or supervisor(s) what you have contributed to the company and will provide in the near future. Depending on the size of the office or team these may be organized by the human resource department or you may need to take the initiative to set up a meeting.

Make sure you are well prepared with specific examples. How and where you have been successful? What do you want to provide moving forward?

You can think of this as re-interviewing for your own job. While that may sound scary it is meant to emphasize the importance of your review and why you are asking for a raise. Generally, you should have this sit down once a year but if there has been a major change in your role or responsibilities it could be sooner.

Remember, just taking up office space and breathing air for a year does not qualify for an increase. Neither does the cost of living or your personal financial situation.

8. Get your license or invest in your education

One of the best places to begin your journey with a high salary is to become licensed. Yes, it is expensive and takes a lot of time but it is very important to advance in the profession.

If you don't believe me just look at the senior members of your or other offices. Are they licensed? Odds are most of them are registered or have a specialty skill. There are exceptions, but it is best to follow a proven path.

Both of these techniques can greatly reduce the time it takes to become licensed. The longer you hold a license generally the more you are worth in the marketplace.

9. Move to an urban area

This may not be the best solution for everyone but since we are putting all the options on the table, this can be the quickest route to a six-figure income. Often by following the population growth, you can take advantage of a hot market looking for talent.

The big benefit of working for an office in a prominent city is that the salary will almost always be higher than the equivalent job in a rural environment. Of course, the reason often cited for this is the higher cost of living.

However, if you are willing to live below your means and skip the penthouse apartment you will be financially better off in the long run. Setting your salary high as early as possible will be a huge advantage throughout your career.

10. Develop multiple income streams

This topic is perhaps my favorite been discussing but if we are strictly talking about breaking the $100k annual figure, it is relevant. I recommend that everyone have multiple income streams. The riskiest position to be in is where one company provides your only source of income. Think about your skill set and what you can do on the side to generate additional income.

There are hundreds of ways to earn additional cash

related to your specific profession. Who knows, that side work may turn out to be even more profitable than your day job.

Pick up freelance work? This can not only provide income in the short term but also create long term connections and contacts. Ultimately, this may lead to additional work or even a more lucrative position.

One note on side jobs, depending on the type of work you are performing your employer's liability insurance can prohibit freelance work, so be sure to do your homework.

Sales growth, gross margins, inventory turns and cash flow captures the status of an enterprise. But to understand how to *improve* a business you have to look beneath the financials---and no one cheat sheet of metrics works for all industries.

Sometimes it's not easy to know which metrics you should be measuring---or how to make use of them. Say you want to learn more about what your customers like or don't. Online surveys are cheap, but gathering meaningful data is tricky. The difference between good data and bad is in how you ask the questions, this is critical in building clientele.

For example, if you ask people if they prefer great quality at a low price, of course, they'll say "Yes"; in reality, though, they may be willing to accept lower quality at a price that still keeps your business in the black. You definitely want to do surveys, whether with your personal career or business.

Your survey does not have to be fancy or super deep. Try using social media to understand what buyers want or look for in the market. Try Starbucks or even the mall and ask random people, what they value more… "Price or Quality!"

"Use fast action to create funds now!" ~LaShanda D. Gary

CHAPTER 5

PLAN

Inspiring vision.

Create a vision so inspiring you can't stop thinking about it. In fact, make it so inspiring it keeps you wide awake at night. Keep your daily focus and thoughts on achieving this vision. Once you have truly sold yourself on your vision that is when the magic starts to happen.

Write down your goals by creating a specific plan inclusive of the exact dates each one will be achieved.

To help you get started right this second, complete my profit plan in the back of this book to increase your productivity plan.

Remember, your vision should resonate with your true passions and must be so compelling that it drives you to action each and every day. Once you have this clear vision in mind, everything else will start falling into place naturally.

Right now, matters.

If you have come this far, you are already ahead of the pack. Now it is time to finish off the competition and distance yourself from others and more importantly from the person you were yesterday. This is one statement I cannot reiterate enough and you must believe it when I tell you that *right now matters*.

You know how short life is, so do not waste your valuable time wallowing or hanging out with those that do. Focus on what you need to accomplish right now to achieve your vision, and make every single minute and each day matter. Track your progress and keep the wheels moving, in doing so mastery can be yours.

I challenge you to forget about the newest luxury handbag, what sports game is on tonight, and what closet you were going to re-arrange, and start producing! If what you are going to do right now does not produce income then do not do it. If you are serious and committed to your success, your next hour, next day, next week, next month, next year, next decade will be focused on these five elements. Once you understand that right now matters, the rest becomes history. I want to help you cut your learning curve in half starting right now.

Produce with excellence.

Having multiple streams of income means that everything I do and put my name to is planned, well-thought-out, and executed with excellence. I refuse to associate my name with anything that is not going to add massive value to my ever-expanding tribe and is not 100 percent congruent with my own vision for my brand. This is why even the free content I make available to all of my loyal fans and followers is produced with excellence and far exceeds the vast majority of paid-for-content put out by others. I make sure everything I do provides phenomenal value for those I impact, customers, and clients. You must do the same.

This dedication to excellence in everything that I do requires that both myself and my team makes every single minute count. There is a purpose for every task I undertake and a specific outcome for everything I do, both personally and professionally. Too many people put their name to the mediocre and insanely useless material because it is easy. Don't do anything because it is easy. Pay attention to everything, you must be detailed oriented, and fiercely selective with what you choose to do and whom you choose to work with. Everything must be cloaked with excellence.

Multiple income streams.

You have your vision and your sense of urgency, now apply that to everything. Not just to your one big idea but to every idea you have. This is where the fun begins. I have to tell you that it is absolutely incredible the number of entrepreneurs, I have met that have built not one but multiple successful businesses in less than 12 months and you can too.

I worked hard to build my own empire and continue to do so each and every day, which as a result, I have had the opportunity to generate multiple streams of income in a wide variety of different types of businesses: The Build a Big Fast Masterclass, Dream Build Success Live Classes, national speaker and mentor, that 'SO FANCY Boutique, GLA Executive Services, G. Services & Design, author of Destiny Strategies for Success and The Path2Purpose Conference along with the Success Conference, contributor to numerous world-class publications, active real estate investor, and the streams go on.

Remember, the golden rule in business: **"Cash flow is King"**. The average millionaire has seven different streams of income. How many do you have?

Sense of urgency.

Once you have your compelling vision, this should come naturally, but cannot be overstated -- do *everything* with a sense of urgency. From taking phone calls to making decisions to creating products and services, if it can be done today, get it done. Period.

Too many people wait on the sidelines to make a decision or make a move. What the hell are you waiting for? The time will *never* be just right. Successful entrepreneurs are always thinking and doing actions that are two steps ahead of their competition. If you are not moving with urgency then you are already ten steps behind. Once you are there, the Holy Grail of entrepreneurship then becomes getting your team to act with this same sense of urgency.

Get them on board your bullet train, not stopping or slowing down for anything or anyone, and mountains can truly be moved.

Complete this ninety-day vision statement. Watch your vision manifest and show gratitude once you celebrate your success.

Are you ready for the ideal ninety vision statement? Complete the next exercise then watch your vision spring forward.

90 Day Vision Statement

_____
_____
_____

What's important to you? In other words, what are your core values? Your values make you do the things that are often not easy to do. You don't want to live life based on somebody else's values.

1. _____

2. _____

3. _____

What are your "BIG 3" for the year? (Top 3 goals within the next 90 days)

1. _____

2. _____

3. _____

What are your 3 most compelling reasons to hit those goals and elevate your life?

1. _____

2. _____

3. _____

What are your key behaviors and habits you must develop?

1. _____

2. _____

3. _____

The exact amount of money you desire by _____, is _____.   You intend to give _____ in return for that money you desire. Your plan of action is _____, _____, _____.

Signature _____

Date _____

CHAPTER 6

GET PAID!

There is nothing more exciting to a visionary than planning, producing, and getting paid for it. Your daily productivity and profit plan is a step by step guide to your day-to day routines and writing practices that have led to my success. Each strategy is created to help you maximize and monetize your brand, business, dreams, and vision.

This is specifically designed to help you plan, produce, and profit to six figures. Whether you're an entrepreneur, student, or career person working your dream job, you definitely want to use these daily productivity practices to get your life and destiny together once and for all.

Plan to Get Paid.

So, if you're struggling with this issue, consider the following 11 tips, including which systems you need to put into place to avoid non-payments and what to do when a client or borrower that flat-out refuses to do the right thing.

Step 1: Set the stage to ensure paying clients.

Before taking on your next customer or client, consider implementing the first two strategies below. These will help ensure you attract those clients who are most likely to pay -- and are the people who understand how you expect to be treated.

Setting healthy boundaries with clients is critical. Ensure you set a clear-cut standard across the board. At first, it may feel a little uneasy, but I am sure you will have no problem with the next juncture.

Raise your rates. Okay, so maybe this tip is a bit counterintuitive, but bear with me. You may believe you can compensate for rock-bottom rates by increased volume. But, trust me when I tell you, this strategy rarely works in the long term. Clients who truly value your services will expect to pay a fair (and sometimes premium) rate and will be unlikely to give you trouble when it comes to making payments.

Have a payment policy in place. Having a payment policy screams "professional" to clients, and helps ensure that you and your clients are on the same page right from the outset. Your policy should cover all aspects of invoicing and collections and explicitly lay out what's included in your rate. Specifics can include:

- How often you'll send invoices
- Payment terms and penalties for late payments
- Your rate structure: for instance, hourly, monthly, per-project, etc.
- Payment methods you'll accept (and won't accept)

- The process you'll follow for late and missed payments

Step 2: Identify deadbeat clients from the outset.

Dealing with late or missing payments can end up costing significant time and money. So, it's always best to identify and weed out potential deadbeats before you even engage with them.

Avoid bargain hunters. You know exactly the kind of client I'm talking about. This is the girl or guy who tries to haggle you down on your rate right from the outset, who says, "You look like the perfect fit, but you're charging 50 percent more than everyone else I've talked to." Assuming you're confident that your rates are fair, don't let these bargain hunters get you down. If they're unhappy with your rates now, think how unhappy they'll be when you send your first invoice.

Be wary of potential clients who don't "get" what you do. Comments like, "Well, I've been told we need your services, but I'm not really sure," should be a major red flag. If they're hesitant that they even need you, they'll be far more likely to argue over or even avoid payments. Stick with clients who know they need you, and know that you're the right person for the job.

Is the client hesitant to sign a contract? RUN. Any reasonable client will be more than happy to sign a contract, especially one that offers standard billing terms. If a potential client seems hesitant to sign (often revealed by the lengthy period taken to sign and return it), RUN. This can be a sign that he or she is anticipating future problems and looking for loopholes.

Get references and credit checks. Many entrepreneurs avoid this important step for fear of appearing paranoid or distrustful. But if you're going to be working with a client for a long time -- or billing this employer for a lot of work -- it's an absolute must. Checking references can be as simple as calling up clients listed on the company website, and running client risk reports through a service like Cortera for as little as $2.50.

Step 3: Collect on overdue accounts.

Despite your best efforts, there will likely come a time when a client will miss a payment deadline. How you react and respond to the situation can make a big difference.

Get in touch immediately. You may be tempted to wait several weeks to follow up with late-paying clients. However, with each passing week, your likelihood of getting paid decreases. Get in touch (preferably by phone) within a few days of the missed payment date, and politely inquire as to the client's expected time line.

After 30 days, start charging interest. Hopefully, your payment policy (see No. 2) specified your terms for overdue payments. Most companies begin charging interest at 30 days past the invoice date; some are even pushing for their fellow freelancers to require immediate payment. Be sure to include your late payment fee on any subsequent invoices you send.

Continue to get in touch. It's sad but true: Some clients will need some significant "nudging" to make a payment. Continue to reach out regularly via phone and email to inquire about the status of payment. Remind the client of the payment terms and indicate the amount of interest that has accrued.

For very late payments, send a demand letter. At a certain point, you'll realize that even if the client does end up paying, he or she will no longer be your client. This is when to draw up a demand letter (or have your lawyer do it), outlining the legal action you'll take if payment isn't received by a certain date.

Hire a collection agency. Because these agencies take a percentage of the debt they collect, this should always be your last resort . . . and should only be used for collecting on large amounts. Keep in mind that most agencies won't take your case unless the payment is at least 90 days overdue.

A last-ditch (controversial) strategy to collect from non-paying clients

As a last resort, try this controversial but effective strategy: Publicly reach out on social media. As I said, this is controversial! While I haven't -- and likely wouldn't ever -- use this strategy, some businesses (Americas Most Wanted List) have used it effectively as a last-ditch effort to collect, especially if the amount owed is substantial.

If your client has failed to respond despite numerous phone calls and the threat of legal action, a simple, "Your invoice is now 90 days late. Please let me know when I can expect payment" on his or her Facebook page or Twitter can be very effective. Keep in mind that this strategy -- while effective - may ultimately hurt your reputation or even result in legal action against you. Through payment research, I found that after 90 days of waiting for a payment, you only have something like a 5 percent chance of getting paid.

Are you ready to write your goals? Complete the following exercises and guide to maximize your profitability. I have consistently completed my profitability plan daily and see the fruits of my labor and you can too.

Productivity Planner

MY TOP 10 GOALS

Set your top 10 major goals every quarter. Review them often and celebrate your success.

1. _____

2. _____

3. _____

4. _____

5. _____

6. _____

7. _____

8. _____

9. _____

10. _____

MY TOP 10 GOALS

Set your top 10 major goals every quarter. Review them often and celebrate your success.

1. _____

2. _____

3. _____

4. _____

5. _____

6. _____

7. _____

8. _____

9. _____

10._____

MY TOP 10 GOALS

Set your top 10 major goals every quarter. Review them often and celebrate your success.

1. _____

2. _____

3. _____

4. _____

5. _____

6. _____

7. _____

8. _____

9. _____

10. _____

MY TOP 10 GOALS

Set your top 10 major goals every quarter. Review them often and celebrate your success.

1. _____

2. _____

3. _____

4. _____

5. _____

6. _____

7. _____

8. _____

9. _____

10. _____

Write Your Success Story

Think ginormous, extraordinary, largescale and write your story. What do you want your story to look like?

_____

_____

_____

_____

_____

_____

_____

_____

_____

_____

_____

_____

_____

Product Launch Plan Summary

This is your high-level overview of your idea launch plan. Using this outline will keep you focused, on track, and activate your success plan.

Launch Goals

Product Summary

Target Buyers

Readiness Assessment

Launch Strategy

Budget

Risks

LAUNCH CHART

Include all functional areas contributing or affected by the launch.

Project/Product/Process	Cost	30 Day Goal	Results
Launch Date			
Product			
Product Marketing			
Development Days			
Time Invested			
Manufacturing Cost			
Marketing Communications			
Social Media			
Public Relations			
Direct Sales			
Customer Support			
Professional Services			
Operations			

Promotions & Product Launches

The following worksheet is simply to act as a guideline to help map out your marketing plans. What product or service will you focus your marketing efforts toward this month? Are you launching a new product or services? Fill in the sections below to help you get your ideas out of your mind and into the marketplace.

Month: _____ **Today's Date:** _____

Name of Product/Program/Service to Promote this month:

_____

DATE TO START PROMOTIONS _____

INCOME GOAL FOR THIS PROMOTION $ _____

TO REACH THIS GOAL, I MUST SELL _____ **(QTY)**

AT $ _____ **(PRICE)**

MARKETING IDEAS:

1. _____

2. _____

3. _____

4. _____

5. _____

6. _____

7. _____

FAVORTIE LESSON FROM THIS LAUNCH: _____

_____.

Promotions & Product Launches

The following worksheet is simply to act as a guideline to help map out your marketing plans. What product or service will you focus your marketing efforts toward this month? Are you launching a new product or services? Fill in the sections below to help you get your ideas out of your mind and into the marketplace.

Month: _____ **Today's Date:** _____

Name of Product/Program/Service to Promote this month:

_____

DATE TO START PROMOTIONS _____

INCOME GOAL FOR THIS PROMOTION $ _____

TO REACH THIS GOAL, I MUST SELL _____ **(QTY) AT $** _____ **(PRICE)**

MARKETING IDEAS:

1. _____

2. _____

3. _____

4. _____

5. _____

6. _____

7. _____

FAVORTIE LESSON FROM THIS LAUNCH: _____

_____.

I Will Reach My Goals in Life and Business

MY PERSONAL GOALS:

1. _____

2. _____

3. _____

4. _____

5. _____

6. _____

7. _____

8. _____

9. _____

10. _____

MY BUSINESS GOALS:

1. _____

2. _____

3. _____

4. _____

5. _____

6. _____

7. _____

8. _____

9. _____

10. _____

"MY SUCCESS STRATEGY PLAN WORKS DAILY!"

Focus Quote

_____

What I've Learned That Has Changed Everything for my family and I

_____

To Do List

_____

_____

_____

Write Your Success Story

Think ginormous, extraordinary, largescale and write your story. What do you want your story to look like?

Product Launch Plan Summary

This is your high-level overview of your idea launch plan. Using this outline will keep you focused, on track, and activate your success plan.

Launch Goals

Product Summary

Target Buyers

Readiness Assessment

Launch Strategy

Budget

Risks

LAUNCH CHART

Include all functional areas contributing or affected by the launch.

Project/Product/Process	Cost	30 Day Goal	Results
Launch Date			
Product			
Product Marketing			
Development Days			
Time Invested			
Manufacturing Cost			
Marketing Communications			
Social Media			
Public Relations			
Direct Sales			
Customer Support			
Professional Services			
Operations			

Promotions & Product Launches

The following worksheet is simply to act as a guideline to help map out your marketing plans. What product or service will you focus your marketing efforts toward this month? Are you launching a new product or services? Fill in the sections below to help you get your ideas out of your mind and into the marketplace.

Month: _____ **Today's Date:** _____

Name of Product/Program/Service to Promote this month:

_____

DATE TO START PROMOTIONS _____

INCOME GOAL FOR THIS PROMOTION $_____

TO REACH THIS GOAL, I MUST SELL _____ **(QTY)**

AT $ _____ **(PRICE)**

MARKETING IDEAS:

1. _____
2. _____
3. _____
4. _____
5. _____
6. _____
7. _____

FAVORTIE LESSON FROM THIS LAUNCH: _____

_____.

Promotions & Product Launches

The following worksheet is simply to act as a guideline to help map out your marketing plans. What product or service will you focus your marketing efforts toward this month? Are you launching a new product or services? Fill in the sections below to help you get your ideas out of your mind and into the marketplace.

Month: _____ **Today's Date:** _____

Name of Product/Program/Service to Promote this month:

_____

DATE TO START PROMOTIONS _____

INCOME GOAL FOR THIS PROMOTION $_____

TO REACH THIS GOAL, I MUST SELL _____ **(QTY) AT $** _____ **(PRICE)**

MARKETING IDEAS:

1. _____

2. _____

3. _____

4. _____

5. _____

6. _____

7. _____

FAVORTIE LESSON FROM THIS LAUNCH: _____

_____.

I Will Reach My Goals in Life and Business

MY PERSONAL GOALS:

1. _____

2. _____

3. _____

4. _____

5. _____

6. _____

7. _____

8. _____

9. _____

10. _____

MY BUSINESS GOALS:

1. _____

2. _____

3. _____

4. _____

5. _____

6. _____

7. _____

8. _____

9. _____

10. _____

"MY SUCCESS STRATEGY PLAN WORKS DAILY!"

Focus Quote

_____

What I've Learned That Has Changed Everything for my family and I

_____

To Do List

_____

_____

_____

Write Your Success Story

Think ginormous, extraordinary, largescale and write your story. What do you want your story to look like?

Product Launch Plan Summary

This is your high-level overview of your idea launch plan. Using this outline will keep you focused, on track, and activate your success plan.

Launch Goals

Product Summary

Target Buyers

Readiness Assessment

Launch Strategy

Budget

Risks

LAUNCH CHART

Include all functional areas contributing or affected by the launch.

Project/Product/Process	Cost	30 Day Goal	Results
Launch Date			
Product			
Product Marketing			
Development Days			
Time Invested			
Manufacturing Cost			
Marketing Communications			
Social Media			
Public Relations			
Direct Sales			
Customer Support			
Professional Services			
Operations			

Promotions & Product Launches

The following worksheet is simply to act as a guideline to help map out your marketing plans. What product or service will you focus your marketing efforts toward this month? Are you launching a new product or services? Fill in the sections below to help you get your ideas out of your mind and into the marketplace.

Month: _____ **Today's Date:** _____

Name of Product/Program/Service to Promote this month:

_____

DATE TO START PROMOTIONS _____

INCOME GOAL FOR THIS PROMOTION $_____

TO REACH THIS GOAL, I MUST SELL _____ **(QTY)**

AT $ _____ **(PRICE)**

MARKETING IDEAS:

1. _____

2. _____

3. _____

4. _____

5. _____

6. _____

7. _____

FAVORTIE LESSON FROM THIS LAUNCH: _____

_____.

Promotions & Product Launches

The following worksheet is simply to act as a guideline to help map out your marketing plans. What product or service will you focus your marketing efforts toward this month? Are you launching a new product or services? Fill in the sections below to help you get your ideas out of your mind and into the marketplace.

Month: _____ **Today's Date:** _____

Name of Product/Program/Service to Promote this month:

_____

DATE TO START PROMOTIONS _____

INCOME GOAL FOR THIS PROMOTION $ _____

TO REACH THIS GOAL, I MUST SELL _____ **(QTY) AT $** _____ **(PRICE)**

MARKETING IDEAS:

1. _____

2. _____

3. _____

4. _____

5. _____

6. _____

7. _____

FAVORTIE LESSON FROM THIS LAUNCH: _____

_____.

I Will Reach My Goals in Life and Business

MY PERSONAL GOALS:

1. _____

2. _____

3. _____

4. _____

5. _____

6. _____

7. _____

8. _____

9. _____

10. _____

MY BUSINESS GOALS:

1. _____

2. _____

3. _____

4. _____

5. _____

6. _____

7. _____

8. _____

9. _____

10. _____

"MY SUCCESS STRATEGY PLAN WORKS DAILY!"

Focus Quote

_____

What I've Learned That Has Changed Everything for my family and I

_____

To Do List

_____

_____

_____

Write Your Success Story

Think ginormous, extraordinary, largescale and write your story. What do you want your story to look like?

_____

_____

_____

_____

_____

_____

_____

_____

_____

_____

_____

_____

_____

Product Launch Plan Summary

This is your high-level overview of your idea launch plan. Using this outline will keep you focused, on track, and activate your success plan.

Launch Goals

Product Summary

Target Buyers

Readiness Assessment

Launch Strategy

Budget

Risks

LAUNCH CHART

Include all functional areas contributing or affected by the launch.

Project/Product/Process	Cost	30 Day Goal	Results
Launch Date			
Product			
Product Marketing			
Development Days			
Time Invested			
Manufacturing Cost			
Marketing Communications			
Social Media			
Public Relations			
Direct Sales			
Customer Support			
Professional Services			
Operations			

Promotions & Product Launches

The following worksheet is simply to act as a guideline to help map out your marketing plans. What product or service will you focus your marketing efforts toward this month? Are you launching a new product or services? Fill in the sections below to help you get your ideas out of your mind and into the marketplace.

Month: _____ **Today's Date:** _____

Name of Product/Program/Service to Promote this month:

_____

DATE TO START PROMOTIONS _____

INCOME GOAL FOR THIS PROMOTION $_____

TO REACH THIS GOAL, I MUST SELL _____ **(QTY)**

AT $ _____ **(PRICE)**

MARKETING IDEAS:

1. _____
2. _____
3. _____
4. _____
5. _____
6. _____
7. _____

FAVORTIE LESSON FROM THIS LAUNCH: _____

_____.

Promotions & Product Launches

The following worksheet is simply to act as a guideline to help map out your marketing plans. What product or service will you focus your marketing efforts toward this month? Are you launching a new product or services? Fill in the sections below to help you get your ideas out of your mind and into the marketplace.

Month: _____ Today's Date: _____

Name of Product/Program/Service to Promote this month:

_____

DATE TO START PROMOTIONS _____

INCOME GOAL FOR THIS PROMOTION $_____

TO REACH THIS GOAL, I MUST SELL _____ (QTY)
AT $ _____ (PRICE)

MARKETING IDEAS:

1. _____

2. _____

3. _____

4. _____

5. _____

6. _____

7. _____

FAVORTIE LESSON FROM THIS LAUNCH: _____

_____.

I Will Reach My Goals in Life and Business

MY PERSONAL GOALS:

1. _____

2. _____

3. _____

4. _____

5. _____

6. _____

7. _____

8._____

9._____

10._____

MY BUSINESS GOALS:

1. _____

2. _____

3. _____

4. _____

5. _____

6. _____

7. _____

8. _____

9. _____

10. _____

"MY SUCCESS STRATEGY PLAN WORKS DAILY!"

Focus Quote

_____

What I've Learned That Has Changed Everything for my family and I

_____

To Do List

_____

_____

_____

Write Your Success Story

Think ginormous, extraordinary, largescale and write your story. What do you want your story to look like?

Product Launch Plan Summary

This is your high-level overview of your idea launch plan. Using this outline will keep you focused, on track, and activate your success plan.

Launch Goals

Product Summary

Target Buyers

Readiness Assessment

Launch Strategy

Budget

Risks

LAUNCH CHART

Include all functional areas contributing or affected by the launch.

Project/Product/Process	Cost	30 Day Goal	Results
Launch Date			
Product			
Product Marketing			
Development Days			
Time Invested			
Manufacturing Cost			
Marketing Communications			
Social Media			
Public Relations			
Direct Sales			
Customer Support			
Professional Services			
Operations			

Promotions & Product Launches

The following worksheet is simply to act as a guideline to help map out your marketing plans. What product or service will you focus your marketing efforts toward this month? Are you launching a new product or services? Fill in the sections below to help you get your ideas out of your mind and into the marketplace.

Month: _____ **Today's Date:** _____

Name of Product/Program/Service to Promote this month:

_____

DATE TO START PROMOTIONS _____

INCOME GOAL FOR THIS PROMOTION $ _____

TO REACH THIS GOAL, I MUST SELL _____ **(QTY)**

AT $ _____ **(PRICE)**

MARKETING IDEAS:

1. _____
2. _____
3. _____
4. _____
5. _____
6. _____
7. _____

FAVORTIE LESSON FROM THIS LAUNCH: _____

_____.

Promotions & Product Launches

The following worksheet is simply to act as a guideline to help map out your marketing plans. What product or service will you focus your marketing efforts toward this month? Are you launching a new product or services? Fill in the sections below to help you get your ideas out of your mind and into the marketplace.

Month: _____ Today's Date: _____

Name of Product/Program/Service to Promote this month:

_____

DATE TO START PROMOTIONS _____

INCOME GOAL FOR THIS PROMOTION $_____

TO REACH THIS GOAL, I MUST SELL _____ (QTY)
AT $ _____ (PRICE)

MARKETING IDEAS:

1. _____

2. _____

3. _____

4. _____

5. _____

6. _____

7. _____

FAVORTIE LESSON FROM THIS LAUNCH: _____

_____.

I Will Reach My Goals in Life and Business

MY PERSONAL GOALS:

1. _____

2. _____

3. _____

4. _____

5. _____

6. _____

7. _____

8._____

9._____

10._____

MY BUSINESS GOALS:

1. _____

2. _____

3. _____

4. _____

5. _____

6. _____

7. _____

8. _____

9. _____

10. _____

"MY SUCCESS STRATEGY PLAN WORKS DAILY!"

Focus Quote

_____

What I've Learned That Has Changed Everything for my family and I

_____

To Do List

_____

_____

_____

Write Your Success Story

Think ginormous, extraordinary, largescale and write your story. What do you want your story to look like?

_____

_____

_____

_____

_____

_____

_____

_____

_____

_____

_____

_____

_____

_____

Product Launch Plan Summary

This is your high-level overview of your idea launch plan. Using this outline will keep you focused, on track, and activate your success plan.

Launch Goals

Product Summary

Target Buyers

Readiness Assessment

Launch Strategy

Budget

Risks

LAUNCH CHART

Include all functional areas contributing or affected by the launch.

Project/Product/Process	Cost	30 Day Goal	Results
Launch Date			
Product			
Product Marketing			
Development Days			
Time Invested			
Manufacturing Cost			
Marketing Communications			
Social Media			
Public Relations			
Direct Sales			
Customer Support			
Professional Services			
Operations			

Promotions & Product Launches

The following worksheet is simply to act as a guideline to help map out your marketing plans. What product or service will you focus your marketing efforts toward this month? Are you launching a new product or services? Fill in the sections below to help you get your ideas out of your mind and into the marketplace.

Month: _____ **Today's Date:** _____

Name of Product/Program/Service to Promote this month:

_____

DATE TO START PROMOTIONS _____

INCOME GOAL FOR THIS PROMOTION $ _____

TO REACH THIS GOAL, I MUST SELL _____ **(QTY)**

AT $ _____ **(PRICE)**

MARKETING IDEAS:

1. _____
2. _____
3. _____
4. _____
5. _____
6. _____
7. _____

FAVORTIE LESSON FROM THIS LAUNCH: _____

_____.

Promotions & Product Launches

The following worksheet is simply to act as a guideline to help map out your marketing plans. What product or service will you focus your marketing efforts toward this month? Are you launching a new product or services? Fill in the sections below to help you get your ideas out of your mind and into the marketplace.

Month: _____ **Today's Date:** _____

Name of Product/Program/Service to Promote this month:

_____

DATE TO START PROMOTIONS _____

INCOME GOAL FOR THIS PROMOTION $ _____

TO REACH THIS GOAL, I MUST SELL _____ **(QTY) AT $** _____ **(PRICE)**

MARKETING IDEAS:

1. _____

2. _____

3. _____

4. _____

5. _____

6. _____

7. _____

FAVORTIE LESSON FROM THIS LAUNCH: _____

_____.

I Will Reach My Goals in Life and Business

MY PERSONAL GOALS:

1. _____

2. _____

3. _____

4. _____

5. _____

6. _____

7. _____

8. _____

9. _____

10. _____

MY BUSINESS GOALS:

1. _____

2. _____

3. _____

4. _____

5. _____

6. _____

7. _____

8. _____

9. _____

10. _____

"MY SUCCESS STRATEGY PLAN WORKS DAILY!"

Focus Quote

_____

What I've Learned That Has Changed Everything for my family and I

_____

To Do List

_____

_____

_____

Write Your Success Story

Think ginormous, extraordinary, largescale and write your story. What do you want your story to look like?

_____

_____

_____

_____

_____

_____

_____

_____

_____

_____

_____

_____

_____

Product Launch Plan Summary

This is your high-level overview of your idea launch plan. Using this outline will keep you focused, on track, and activate your success plan.

Launch Goals

Product Summary

Target Buyers

Readiness Assessment

Launch Strategy

Budget

Risks

LAUNCH CHART

Include all functional areas contributing or affected by the launch.

Project/Product/Process	Cost	30 Day Goal	Results
Launch Date			
Product			
Product Marketing			
Development Days			
Time Invested			
Manufacturing Cost			
Marketing Communications			
Social Media			
Public Relations			
Direct Sales			
Customer Support			
Professional Services			
Operations			

Promotions & Product Launches

The following worksheet is simply to act as a guideline to help map out your marketing plans. What product or service will you focus your marketing efforts toward this month? Are you launching a new product or services? Fill in the sections below to help you get your ideas out of your mind and into the marketplace.

Month: _____ **Today's Date:** _____

Name of Product/Program/Service to Promote this month:

_____

DATE TO START PROMOTIONS _____

INCOME GOAL FOR THIS PROMOTION $_____

TO REACH THIS GOAL, I MUST SELL _____ **(QTY)**

AT $ _____ **(PRICE)**

MARKETING IDEAS:

1. _____

2. _____

3. _____

4. _____

5. _____

6. _____

7. _____

FAVORTIE LESSON FROM THIS LAUNCH: _____

_____.

Promotions & Product Launches

The following worksheet is simply to act as a guideline to help map out your marketing plans. What product or service will you focus your marketing efforts toward this month? Are you launching a new product or services? Fill in the sections below to help you get your ideas out of your mind and into the marketplace.

Month: _____ **Today's Date:** _____

Name of Product/Program/Service to Promote this month:

_____

DATE TO START PROMOTIONS _____

INCOME GOAL FOR THIS PROMOTION $_____

TO REACH THIS GOAL, I MUST SELL _____ **(QTY) AT $** _____ **(PRICE)**

MARKETING IDEAS:

1. _____

2. _____

3. _____

4. _____

5. _____

6. _____

7. _____

FAVORTIE LESSON FROM THIS LAUNCH: _____

_____.

I Will Reach My Goals in Life and Business

MY PERSONAL GOALS:

1. _____

2. _____

3. _____

4. _____

5. _____

6. _____

7. _____

8. _____

9. _____

10. _____

MY BUSINESS GOALS:

1. _____

2. _____

3. _____

4. _____

5. _____

6. _____

7. _____

8. _____

9. _____

10. _____

"MY SUCCESS STRATEGY PLAN WORKS DAILY!"

Focus Quote

_____

What I've Learned That Has Changed Everything for my family and I

_____

To Do List

_____

_____

_____

Write Your Success Story

Think ginormous, extraordinary, largescale and write your story. What do you want your story to look like?

Product Launch Plan Summary

This is your high-level overview of your idea launch plan. Using this outline will keep you focused, on track, and activate your success plan.

Launch Goals

Product Summary

Target Buyers

Readiness Assessment

Launch Strategy

Budget

Risks

LAUNCH CHART

Include all functional areas contributing or affected by the launch.

Project/Product/Process	Cost	30 Day Goal	Results
Launch Date			
Product			
Product Marketing			
Development Days			
Time Invested			
Manufacturing Cost			
Marketing Communications			
Social Media			
Public Relations			
Direct Sales			
Customer Support			
Professional Services			
Operations			

Promotions & Product Launches

The following worksheet is simply to act as a guideline to help map out your marketing plans. What product or service will you focus your marketing efforts toward this month? Are you launching a new product or services? Fill in the sections below to help you get your ideas out of your mind and into the marketplace.

Month: _____ Today's Date: _____

Name of Product/Program/Service to Promote this month:

_____

DATE TO START PROMOTIONS _____

INCOME GOAL FOR THIS PROMOTION $_____

TO REACH THIS GOAL, I MUST SELL _____ **(QTY)**

AT $ _____ **(PRICE)**

MARKETING IDEAS:

1. _____

2. _____

3. _____

4. _____

5. _____

6. _____

7. _____

FAVORTIE LESSON FROM THIS LAUNCH: _____

_____.

Promotions & Product Launches

The following worksheet is simply to act as a guideline to help map out your marketing plans. What product or service will you focus your marketing efforts toward this month? Are you launching a new product or services? Fill in the sections below to help you get your ideas out of your mind and into the marketplace.

Month: _____ **Today's Date:** _____

Name of Product/Program/Service to Promote this month:

_____

DATE TO START PROMOTIONS _____

INCOME GOAL FOR THIS PROMOTION $ _____

TO REACH THIS GOAL, I MUST SELL _____ **(QTY)**
AT $ _____ **(PRICE)**

MARKETING IDEAS:

1. _____

2. _____

3. _____

4. _____

5. _____

6. _____

7. _____

FAVORTIE LESSON FROM THIS LAUNCH: _____

_____.

I Will Reach My Goals in Life and Business

MY PERSONAL GOALS:

1. _____

2. _____

3. _____

4. _____

5. _____

6. _____

7. _____

8. _____

9. _____

10. _____

MY BUSINESS GOALS:

1. _____

2. _____

3. _____

4. _____

5. _____

6. _____

7. _____

8. _____

9. _____

10. _____

"MY SUCCESS STRATEGY PLAN WORKS DAILY!"

Focus Quote

What I've Learned That Has Changed Everything for my family and I

To Do List

Write Your Success Story

Think ginormous, extraordinary, largescale and write your story. What do you want your story to look like?

_____

_____

_____

_____

_____

_____

_____

_____

_____

_____

_____

_____

Product Launch Plan Summary

This is your high-level overview of your idea launch plan. Using this outline will keep you focused, on track, and activate your success plan.

Launch Goals

Product Summary

Target Buyers

Readiness Assessment

Launch Strategy

Budget

Risks

LAUNCH CHART

Include all functional areas contributing or affected by the launch.

Project/Product/Process	Cost	30 Day Goal	Results
Launch Date			
Product			
Product Marketing			
Development Days			
Time Invested			
Manufacturing Cost			
Marketing Communications			
Social Media			
Public Relations			
Direct Sales			
Customer Support			
Professional Services			
Operations			

Promotions & Product Launches

The following worksheet is simply to act as a guideline to help map out your marketing plans. What product or service will you focus your marketing efforts toward this month? Are you launching a new product or services? Fill in the sections below to help you get your ideas out of your mind and into the marketplace.

Month: _____ **Today's Date:** _____

Name of Product/Program/Service to Promote this month:

_____

DATE TO START PROMOTIONS _____

INCOME GOAL FOR THIS PROMOTION $_____

TO REACH THIS GOAL, I MUST SELL _____ **(QTY)**

AT $ _____ **(PRICE)**

MARKETING IDEAS:

1. _____

2. _____

3. _____

4. _____

5. _____

6. _____

7. _____

FAVORTIE LESSON FROM THIS LAUNCH: _____

_____.

Promotions & Product Launches

The following worksheet is simply to act as a guideline to help map out your marketing plans. What product or service will you focus your marketing efforts toward this month? Are you launching a new product or services? Fill in the sections below to help you get your ideas out of your mind and into the marketplace.

Month: _____ **Today's Date:** _____

Name of Product/Program/Service to Promote this month:

_____

DATE TO START PROMOTIONS _____

INCOME GOAL FOR THIS PROMOTION $ _____

TO REACH THIS GOAL, I MUST SELL _____ **(QTY) AT $** _____ **(PRICE)**

MARKETING IDEAS:

1. _____

2. _____

3. _____

4. _____

5. _____

6. _____

7. _____

FAVORTIE LESSON FROM THIS LAUNCH: _____

_____.

I Will Reach My Goals in Life and Business

MY PERSONAL GOALS:

1. _____

2. _____

3. _____

4. _____

5. _____

6. _____

7. _____

8. _____

9. _____

10. _____

MY BUSINESS GOALS:

1. _____

2. _____

3. _____

4. _____

5. _____

6. _____

7. _____

8. _____

9. _____

10. _____

"MY SUCCESS STRATEGY PLAN WORKS DAILY!"

Focus Quote

_____

What I've Learned That Has Changed Everything for my family and I

_____

To Do List

_____

_____

_____

Write Your Success Story

Think ginormous, extraordinary, largescale and write your story. What do you want your story to look like?

_____

_____

_____

_____

_____

_____

_____

_____

_____

_____

_____

_____

_____

_____

Product Launch Plan Summary

This is your high-level overview of your idea launch plan. Using this outline will keep you focused, on track, and activate your success plan.

Launch Goals

Product Summary

Target Buyers

Readiness Assessment

Launch Strategy

Budget

Risks

LAUNCH CHART

Include all functional areas contributing or affected by the launch.

Project/Product/Process	Cost	30 Day Goal	Results
Launch Date			
Product			
Product Marketing			
Development Days			
Time Invested			
Manufacturing Cost			
Marketing Communications			
Social Media			
Public Relations			
Direct Sales			
Customer Support			
Professional Services			
Operations			

Promotions & Product Launches

The following worksheet is simply to act as a guideline to help map out your marketing plans. What product or service will you focus your marketing efforts toward this month? Are you launching a new product or services? Fill in the sections below to help you get your ideas out of your mind and into the marketplace.

Month: _____ **Today's Date:** _____

Name of Product/Program/Service to Promote this month:

_____

DATE TO START PROMOTIONS _____

INCOME GOAL FOR THIS PROMOTION $_____

TO REACH THIS GOAL, I MUST SELL _____ **(QTY)**

AT $ _____ **(PRICE)**

MARKETING IDEAS:

1. _____
2. _____
3. _____
4. _____
5. _____
6. _____
7. _____

FAVORTIE LESSON FROM THIS LAUNCH: _____

_____.

Promotions & Product Launches

The following worksheet is simply to act as a guideline to help map out your marketing plans. What product or service will you focus your marketing efforts toward this month? Are you launching a new product or services? Fill in the sections below to help you get your ideas out of your mind and into the marketplace.

Month: _____ **Today's Date:** _____

Name of Product/Program/Service to Promote this month:

_____

DATE TO START PROMOTIONS _____

INCOME GOAL FOR THIS PROMOTION $_____

TO REACH THIS GOAL, I MUST SELL _____ **(QTY) AT $** _____ **(PRICE)**

MARKETING IDEAS:

1. _____

2. _____

3. _____

4. _____

5. _____

6. _____

7. _____

FAVORTIE LESSON FROM THIS LAUNCH: _____

_____.

I Will Reach My Goals in Life and Business

MY PERSONAL GOALS:

1. _____

2. _____

3. _____

4. _____

5. _____

6. _____

7. _____

8. _____

9. _____

10. _____

MY BUSINESS GOALS:

1. _____

2. _____

3. _____

4. _____

5. _____

6. _____

7. _____

8. _____

9. _____

10. _____

"MY SUCCESS STRATEGY PLAN WORKS DAILY!"

Focus Quote

_____

What I've Learned That Has Changed Everything for my family and I

_____

To Do List

_____

_____

_____

Write Your Success Story

Think ginormous, extraordinary, largescale and write your story. What do you want your story to look like?

_____

_____

_____

_____

_____

_____

_____

_____

_____

_____

_____

_____

_____

_____

Product Launch Plan Summary

This is your high-level overview of your idea launch plan. Using this outline will keep you focused, on track, and activate your success plan.

Launch Goals

Product Summary

Target Buyers

Readiness Assessment

Launch Strategy

Budget

Risks

LAUNCH CHART

Include all functional areas contributing or affected by the launch.

Project/Product/Process	Cost	30 Day Goal	Results
Launch Date			
Product			
Product Marketing			
Development Days			
Time Invested			
Manufacturing Cost			
Marketing Communications			
Social Media			
Public Relations			
Direct Sales			
Customer Support			
Professional Services			
Operations			

Promotions & Product Launches

The following worksheet is simply to act as a guideline to help map out your marketing plans. What product or service will you focus your marketing efforts toward this month? Are you launching a new product or services? Fill in the sections below to help you get your ideas out of your mind and into the marketplace.

Month: _____ **Today's Date:** _____

Name of Product/Program/Service to Promote this month:

_____

DATE TO START PROMOTIONS _____

INCOME GOAL FOR THIS PROMOTION $ _____

TO REACH THIS GOAL, I MUST SELL _____ **(QTY)**

AT $ _____ **(PRICE)**

MARKETING IDEAS:

1. _____

2. _____

3. _____

4. _____

5. _____

6. _____

7. _____

FAVORTIE LESSON FROM THIS LAUNCH: _____

_____.

Promotions & Product Launches

The following worksheet is simply to act as a guideline to help map out your marketing plans. What product or service will you focus your marketing efforts toward this month? Are you launching a new product or services? Fill in the sections below to help you get your ideas out of your mind and into the marketplace.

Month: _____ **Today's Date:** _____

Name of Product/Program/Service to Promote this month:

_____

DATE TO START PROMOTIONS _____

INCOME GOAL FOR THIS PROMOTION $ _____

TO REACH THIS GOAL, I MUST SELL _____ **(QTY) AT $** _____ **(PRICE)**

MARKETING IDEAS:

1. _____

2. _____

3. _____

4. _____

5. _____

6. _____

7. _____

FAVORTIE LESSON FROM THIS LAUNCH: _____

_____.

I Will Reach My Goals in Life and Business

MY PERSONAL GOALS:

1. _____

2. _____

3. _____

4. _____

5. _____

6. _____

7. _____

8. _____

9. _____

10. _____

MY BUSINESS GOALS:

1. _____

2. _____

3. _____

4. _____

5. _____

6. _____

7. _____

8. _____

9. _____

10. _____

"MY SUCCESS STRATEGY PLAN WORKS DAILY!"

Focus Quote

_____

What I've Learned That Has Changed Everything for my family and I

_____

To Do List

_____

_____

_____

Write Your Success Story

Think ginormous, extraordinary, largescale and write your story. What do you want your story to look like?

Product Launch Plan Summary

This is your high-level overview of your idea launch plan. Using this outline will keep you focused, on track, and activate your success plan.

Launch Goals

Product Summary

Target Buyers

Readiness Assessment

Launch Strategy

Budget

Risks

LAUNCH CHART

Include all functional areas contributing or affected by the launch.

Project/Product/Process	Cost	30 Day Goal	Results
Launch Date			
Product			
Product Marketing			
Development Days			
Time Invested			
Manufacturing Cost			
Marketing Communications			
Social Media			
Public Relations			
Direct Sales			
Customer Support			
Professional Services			
Operations			

Promotions & Product Launches

The following worksheet is simply to act as a guideline to help map out your marketing plans. What product or service will you focus your marketing efforts toward this month? Are you launching a new product or services? Fill in the sections below to help you get your ideas out of your mind and into the marketplace.

Month: _____ **Today's Date:** _____

Name of Product/Program/Service to Promote this month:

_____

DATE TO START PROMOTIONS _____

INCOME GOAL FOR THIS PROMOTION $ _____

TO REACH THIS GOAL, I MUST SELL _____ **(QTY)**

AT $ _____ **(PRICE)**

MARKETING IDEAS:

1. _____

2. _____

3. _____

4. _____

5. _____

6. _____

7. _____

FAVORTIE LESSON FROM THIS LAUNCH: _____

_____.

Promotions & Product Launches

The following worksheet is simply to act as a guideline to help map out your marketing plans. What product or service will you focus your marketing efforts toward this month? Are you launching a new product or services? Fill in the sections below to help you get your ideas out of your mind and into the marketplace.

Month: _____ **Today's Date:** _____

Name of Product/Program/Service to Promote this month:

_____

DATE TO START PROMOTIONS _____

INCOME GOAL FOR THIS PROMOTION $ _____

TO REACH THIS GOAL, I MUST SELL _____ **(QTY) AT $** _____ **(PRICE)**

MARKETING IDEAS:

1. _____

2. _____

3. _____

4. _____

5. _____

6. _____

7. _____

FAVORTIE LESSON FROM THIS LAUNCH: _____

_____.

I Will Reach My Goals in Life and Business

MY PERSONAL GOALS:

1. _____

2. _____

3. _____

4. _____

5. _____

6. _____

7. _____

8. _____

9. _____

10. _____

MY BUSINESS GOALS:

1. _____

2. _____

3. _____

4. _____

5. _____

6. _____

7. _____

8. _____

9. _____

10. _____

"MY SUCCESS STRATEGY PLAN WORKS DAILY!"

Focus Quote

_____

What I've Learned That Has Changed Everything for my family and I

_____

To Do List

_____

_____

_____

Write Your Success Story

Think ginormous, extraordinary, largescale and write your story. What do you want your story to look like?

_____

_____

_____

_____

_____

_____

_____

_____

_____

_____

_____

_____

Product Launch Plan Summary

This is your high-level overview of your idea launch plan. Using this outline will keep you focused, on track, and activate your success plan.

Launch Goals

Product Summary

Target Buyers

Readiness Assessment

Launch Strategy

Budget

Risks

LAUNCH CHART

Include all functional areas contributing or affected by the launch.

Project/Product/Process	Cost	30 Day Goal	Results
Launch Date			
Product			
Product Marketing			
Development Days			
Time Invested			
Manufacturing Cost			
Marketing Communications			
Social Media			
Public Relations			
Direct Sales			
Customer Support			
Professional Services			
Operations			

Promotions & Product Launches

The following worksheet is simply to act as a guideline to help map out your marketing plans. What product or service will you focus your marketing efforts toward this month? Are you launching a new product or services? Fill in the sections below to help you get your ideas out of your mind and into the marketplace.

Month: _____ **Today's Date:** _____

Name of Product/Program/Service to Promote this month:

_____

DATE TO START PROMOTIONS _____

INCOME GOAL FOR THIS PROMOTION $ _____

TO REACH THIS GOAL, I MUST SELL _____ **(QTY)**

AT $ _____ **(PRICE)**

MARKETING IDEAS:

1. _____
2. _____
3. _____
4. _____
5. _____
6. _____
7. _____

FAVORTIE LESSON FROM THIS LAUNCH: _____

_____.

Promotions & Product Launches

The following worksheet is simply to act as a guideline to help map out your marketing plans. What product or service will you focus your marketing efforts toward this month? Are you launching a new product or services? Fill in the sections below to help you get your ideas out of your mind and into the marketplace.

Month: _____ **Today's Date:** _____

Name of Product/Program/Service to Promote this month:

_____

DATE TO START PROMOTIONS _____

INCOME GOAL FOR THIS PROMOTION $ _____

TO REACH THIS GOAL, I MUST SELL _____ **(QTY) AT $** _____ **(PRICE)**

MARKETING IDEAS:

1. _____

2. _____

3. _____

4. _____

5. _____

6. _____

7. _____

FAVORTIE LESSON FROM THIS LAUNCH: _____

_____.

I Will Reach My Goals in Life and Business

MY PERSONAL GOALS:

1. _____

2. _____

3. _____

4. _____

5. _____

6. _____

7. _____

8. _____

9. _____

10. _____

MY BUSINESS GOALS:

1. _____

2. _____

3. _____

4. _____

5. _____

6. _____

7. _____

8. _____

9. _____

10. _____

"MY SUCCESS STRATEGY PLAN WORKS DAILY!"

Focus Quote

_____

What I've Learned That Has Changed Everything for my family and I

_____

To Do List

_____

_____

_____

DREAM BUILD SUCCESS NOTES

SUCCESS NOTES

SUCCESS NOTES

SUCCESS NOTES

SUCCESS NOTES

SUCCESS NOTES

SUCCESS NOTES

SUCCESS NOTES

SUCCESS NOTES

SUCCESS NOTES

SUCCESS NOTES

SUCCESS NOTES

SUCCESS NOTES

REFERENCES

"Statistics and Business Quotes from CEO's" © *Forbes.com,* 2015. Web. 22 June 2016.

"Statistics and Reference for Quarterly Sales" © *Entreprenuer.com,* 2015. Web. 27 Aug 2016.

"Definitions" *Version.* © 1973, 1978, 1984 Print.

"Definitions" *The Merriam Webster Dictionary,* © 2016 Merriam-Webster, Web, Incorporated 2016.

Scripture taken from the HOLY BIBLE, NEW INTERNATIONAL VERSION®. Copyright © 1973, 1978, 1984 International Bible Society. Computer file.

ABOUT THE AUTHOR

Award Winning Entrepreneur, Business Strategist, Author, Keynote Speaker, CEO and Founder of Dream Build Success.

Your first encounter with this dynamic entrepreneur is guaranteed to be a whirlwind of passion, excitement and motivation bundled up into a highly-charged business woman, paving the way for the limitless success of her clients.

She believes that everyone should activate their gift from God. She started developing products out of her need as her family, business, and faith expanded. The idea of having a business and brand built around God is her VISION.

A living example of success, Gary has hosted life changing empowerment sessions selling out in less than seventy-two hours. Turning your passions into paychecks, enabling her to motivate fellow entrepreneurs globally. Gary has worked with everyone from the Political elite, to Medical- and National-winners, to, several successful business owners, lawyers, doctors and government officials throughout the United States.

With the use of straight-to-the-point, candid stories and highly charged anecdotes, she inspires people globally to find their inner 'Dream Driver'. Regardless of the goal, Gary focuses her unwavering dedication to empower young girls and women to freely and smartly chase their greatest desires with confidence and knowledge. She frequently partners with outstanding foundations, church groups, youth programs, and entrepreneurs.

She has been featured on magazine covers, KYND Radio, 92.1 Radio One, Women Empowering Change Excellence Award, Smart Girl Foundation Icon Award, Queen B Magazine Entrepreneur of the Month, Black Business Focus Group Hall of Fame, LMP Magazine, BBU Magazine for Women Empowering Change, voted the Top 40/40 in Houston, Texas by i10 Media Group, and currently a contributing writer for NO COMPROMISE Magazine and NCO Blog.

With books, newsletters, retail products, appearances and countless online outlets as part of her growing empire, Gary is able to inspire over 70,000 people yearly and shows no signs of slowing down. She native of Columbus, Texas and currently lives in South Texas with her husband, Abret Gary.

LASHANDA D. GARY — Stay Connected!

CREATOR OF:

GservicesDesign.com, Founder and CEO

In Works Tax Services South Texas, LLC, CFO

GLA Executive Services, LLC, Founder and CEO

DreamBuildSuccess.com, Founder and CEO

Success Coaching Program

22K in 30 Days

Success Conference – Host

Path2Purpose Summit – Host

Destiny: Strategies for Success - Author

SOCIAL MEDIA:

Contact LaShanda at: **info@glaservice.com**

Website: **www.DreamBuildSuccess.com**

Social Media: **@lashandagary**

Made in the USA
Columbia, SC
24 July 2021